T0162389

BOOK OF
TWILIGHT

CREPUSCULARIO

PABLO NERUDA

BOOK OF TWILIGHT

TRANSLATED BY WILLIAM O'DALY

COPPER CANYON PRESS
PORT TOWNSEND, WASHINGTON

Copper Canyon Press is in residence at Fort Worden State Park
in Port Townsend, Washington, under the auspices of Centrum.
Centrum is a gathering place for artists and creative thinkers from
around the world, students of all ages and backgrounds, and
audiences seeking extraordinary cultural enrichment.

LIBRARY OF CONGRESS CATALOGING-IN-PUBLICATION DATA

Names: Neruda, Pablo, 1904–1973, author. | O'Daly, William, translator.
Title: Book of twilight / Pablo Neruda ; translated by William O'Daly.
Description: Port Townsend, Washington : Copper Canyon Press, [2017]
Identifiers: LCCN 2017022735 | ISBN 9781556593987 (hardcover)
Subjects: | BISAC: POETRY / Caribbean & Latin American.
Classification: LCC PQ8097.N4 A2 2017 | DDC 861/.62—dc23
LC record available at https://lccn.loc.gov/2017022735

98765432 FIRST PRINTING

COPPER CANYON PRESS
Post Office Box 271
Port Townsend, Washington 98368
www.coppercanyonpress.org

Contents

THE TWILIGHTS OF MARURI

WINDOW ON THE ROAD

PELLEAS AND MELISANDA

END

TRANSLATOR'S ACKNOWLEDGMENTS

My gratitude alone cannot adequately express the pleasure of working with the poet and Spanish-language editor Paco Márquez, whose appreciation of Neruda and dedication to building cultural bridges benefited the translation. Michael Wiegers, editor-in-chief at Copper Canyon Press, was kind enough to invite me to translate *Crepusculario*. This is the first time the press has proposed that I translate a specific book of Neruda's, after the eight they have previously published, and I deeply appreciate the invitation and the fortuitous timing. Tonaya Craft, managing editor at the press, could not have been more welcoming or more devoted to the best presentation of this work. I extend my heartfelt thanks to the entire staff at Copper Canyon for their excellent support in all matters, as well as to editor Alison Lockhart for her discerning eye. The remarkable David Caligiuri helped to bring out the best in the work. I also wish to thank Kristine Iwersen O'Daly, for her thoughtful counsel and encouragement, and other family and friends who proffered various forms of sustenance: Madeline M. and William L. O'Daly, Kyra O'Daly, JS Graustein, Sam Hamill, Tree Swenson, Eleanor Wilner, John Balaban, Philip Levine, Shaun Griffin, Kathryn Hunt, Zachary Marcus, and Francisco Guzman. Many inspired the desire to translate *Crepusculario,* and I can only hope that this translation of Neruda's beginnings will inspire them in return. Any errors in the translation are solely my own.

INTRODUCTION

From his small, shabby room at 513 Maruri Street, sixteen-year-old Pablo Neruda watched the sunset blaze across the western mountains, the "glorious sheaves of colors" and "scattered arrays of light" lingering in the Santiago sky. The tall, melancholy, consumptive-looking poet who dressed in black had arrived by train from the south of Chile in March 1921. He had been raised in the frontier town of Temuco by a stern railroad-worker father and a quiet, loving stepmother. As a boy, he had been sickly and spent much time in his room—reading, writing, listening to the rain on the roof. As he grew stronger, he felt best roaming in the woods, collecting pinecones, small stones, autumn leaves, and fallen feathers, or among Mapuche blankets covered with baskets, weavings, and other wares at the outdoor market. At age fifteen, he was inspired and guided by the educator and rising star of a poet Gabriela Mistral. Neruda steeped himself in the work of Baudelaire, Rimbaud, Verlaine, Proust, Chekhov, Tolstoy, Dostoyevsky, and Whitman, as well as many others who left lasting impressions. He gained recognition as a fledgling poet and wrote copiously in notebooks, from which some of the poems in Crepusculario later came.

In the year before Neruda arrived in Santiago, student and worker riots against the economic and social policies of the Chilean oligarchy—coupled with the government's sometimes careful, often brutal response—had left their desperate mark. After a long and bitter presidential election process decided by tribunal, the Liberal Alliance coalition's Arturo Alessandri had become the first Chilean president to hail from the middle class. Hope prevailed but the oligarchy still controlled Congress, and much work lay ahead. Neruda preferred listening to the speeches of well-regarded anarchists over attending classes at the Pedagogical Institute, where he was studying to become a teacher of French. He expressed his growing political awareness and commitment to economic and social justice by publishing a regular column in the magazine Claridad, and there he also published his poems. Mayakovsky, Pushkin, and Éluard were among his major influences during this period; above all, he adored Éluard for the humanity of his surrealism. Only later, after Neruda's experiences in Madrid at the onset of the Spanish Civil War, and most notably the execution by Falangists of his good friend Federico García Lorca, would poetry and politics fully weave together in his heart and mind. In Crepusculario, politics—in the usual sense—rarely breaks the surface.

Perhaps the political struggle, the need to find solidarity and to plant one's feet on the ground and in the imagination, contributed to the concurrent reawakening to poetry in Chile. It might have been happening for a decade or more when Neruda found a vibrant community of young poets and writers in Santiago. He had known a few of them in the south, and he relished the companionship and the conversation—the discussions of politics, literary movements, and authors; the sharing of particularly poignant pages of their favorite books; and the recitation to one another of the most captivating lines of their favorite poets. None of them had much money. Yet there often was enough for some wine to help fuel the conversation late into the night. The timid poet, to the disbelief of his companions, did quite well with the young women. He had at least two significant love relationships and perhaps a third, as well as many casual affairs. His friends concluded that those relationships, fleeting or sustained, could only have been sparked by the allure of his poetry.

Love is an ever-present theme in *Crepusculario,* and in some senses the politics of love pervades companion themes—inner passion and vision; spirituality and God; materialism and its vulgarities; beauty and nostalgia; age and aging; the nature of creation and the pain of separation; the youth of his poetry and the torturous provisos of personal and artistic growth. These themes reveal the influence of Latin American *modernismo* on this 1923 volume, a few years after the movement itself had waned. So do the lush, carefully crafted surfaces of the poems, the traces of European Romanticism and Symbolism, the sometimes Parnassian tone, and even the imagery of castle intrigue, princess, and the exotic. Neruda greatly admired two of *modernismo*'s most influential practitioners, Nicaraguan poet Rubén Darío and Cuban poet and revolutionary José Martí. In his memoirs, Neruda calls Darío "one of the most creative poets in the Spanish language." In his poems, Neruda shares many of Martí's values and philosophical perspectives on the vagaries of life and the world. In later work, he expresses his admiration for Martí's commitment to the Cuban Revolution and to the nexus between poetry and politics.

On the other hand, the perfectly tuned and orchestrated music of *Crepusculario* is more traditional than the rich, highly stylized modes typical of modernismo. Tones of melancholy ebb and flow throughout the book, anchored by the poem "Saudade," a Portuguese term referring to a state of longing accompanied by loneliness and a sense of being incomplete. Most apt for Neruda's use of the term might be the seventeenth-century aristocratic soldier-poet Manuel de Melo's oft-quoted definition: "a pleasure you suffer, an ailment you enjoy." In this first book, Neruda's poetic sensibility and voice are already unique. The surrealism is deeply rooted in his experiences of the natural world, in the physical senses, and at times in startling self-awareness, with strong, unabashed humanity at its core.

In remarkably bold and honest terms, *Crepusculario* integrates Neruda's most compelling influences while reprising some of *modernismo*'s more recognizable characteristics. The first section begins by invoking Helios, Greek personification of the sun, with the Titan at the reins of the chariot that each day crosses the sky to Oceanus as Oceanus circles the earth. The poem "Pantheos" calls to mind the view that the universe and God are one and the same. All things are divine. The title "Pantheos" seems to indicate that which gives all things their identity, in their suffering and their mortality, announcing the solidarity that makes them what they are and links them to other identities. "New Sonnet for Helen" turns the Romanticism of Pierre de Ronsard, drunk with love for Hélène, on its head. Neruda remarks, "only once do flowers give off their essence," as he imagines the process by which he will be left holding the pain and the grief with which he once filled her. She will come to understand that the snows of spring are harsher. In a final example, the poem "Ivresse" mixes the love of a woman with an exalted state of drunkenness, in which we "escape being the martyred slaves of time," as Baudelaire described *ivresse*. The poem begins by invoking the passion of the apostle Paul, who dedicated his life to expressing gratitude for everything that led to his transformation, including the privations and the pain.

The fifth section, "Pelleas and Melisanda," is based on the Symbolist play by Maurice Maeterlinck, a Belgian playwright, poet, and essayist who wrote in French. The play, which later was adapted as an opera by Claude Debussy, is based on a complicated love triangle involving Golaud, the grandson of the king; the mysterious woman Melisanda, whom Golaud finds crying beside a forest spring; and Golaud's half brother, Pelleas, who convinces the king to allow Golaud to marry Melisanda. But then, as Pelleas and Melisanda grow closer and fall in love, they begin the inexorable slide toward their doom. In "The Wondrous Conversation," Pelleas's words foreshadow the fall, and in so doing encapsulate Neruda's perspective on love and memory:

> One of your smiles erases an entire past:
> may your sweet lips keep what's now far away.

To pay for the publication of his first book, Neruda sold his few pieces of furniture and pawned the watch his father had given him as a parting gift, as well as his black "poet's suit," cape and all. Another, surprising source of funds was the right-wing critic Hernán Díaz Arrieta, who would later savage Neruda in print. The celebrated, flamboyant anarchist Juan Gandulfo, to whom *Crepusculario* is dedicated, provided the wood engravings for the illustrations. In *Memoirs*, Neruda describes what it was like to hold the book in his hands:

> I don't believe any craftsman except the poet, still shaken by the confusion of his dreams, ever experiences the ecstasy produced only once in his life, by the first object his hands have created. It's a moment that will never come back.... But that moment when the first book appears with its ink fresh and its paper still crisp, that enchanted and ecstatic moment, with the sound of wings beating or the first flower opening on the conquered height, that moment comes only once in the poet's lifetime.

Chilean readers embraced the book, and it was mostly well received by critics, some sensing that a great talent had been born. In the streets of Santiago, young people would recite passages from "Farewell," the only poem in the book with a title in English, perhaps echoing Symbolist poet Verlaine's use of an English title, "Nevermore," for a single poem in his first book, *Poèmes saturniens* (1866). "Farewell" captures fleeting and lasting elements of love, and an inescapable separation made sweet by memory, in one of the most beautiful, lyrical poems in the book:

> No longer will my eyes savor your eyes,
> no longer will my pain grow sweeter beside you.
>
> But wherever I go I will take your gaze,
> wherever you walk you will take my pain.

As with the work of any master poet, particularly one as influential and treasured worldwide as Neruda, English speakers' understanding is deepened and broadened, our lives enriched, by having all of the work translated into English. Whether that dream of complete translation for Neruda's work comes true, this book establishes the poet's inimitable voice and belongs in the English-language canon. I first considered translating the book while setting aside, in the late 1970s, the manuscript of *Still Another Day* (*Aún*), my first book of Neruda translation. Daunting challenges of syntax and tone were an attraction and a warning, but I was not able to feel the book in English. In early 2016, as I prepared to translate *Crepusculario*, which Neruda published when he was nineteen years old, I was drawn to explore the symmetry of having first attempted to translate Neruda's work when I was a nineteen-year-old student of English at University of California–Santa Barbara. I went on to translate eight of Neruda's late-career and posthumous books. At this writing I am in my sixties, about the age Neruda was when he published the earliest of those late-career books, *Las manos del día* (*The Hands of Day*). It seems fitting that I only now translate "the first roses—fellow traveler—of [his] inconsolable adolescent garden" ("Beginning").

I am glad to have waited until I could hear the voice of my own beginnings in this book and translate, as an old soul, the "lost crazy words" of the emerging poet, primal in his honesty and brilliant in his vision.

WILLIAM O'DALY
MARCH 2017

BOOK OF
TWILIGHT

CREPUSCULARIO

HELIOS

HELIOS

INICIAL

He ido bajo Helios, que me mira sangrante
laborando en silencio mis jardines ausentes.

Mi voz será la misma del sembrador que cante
cuando bote a los surcos siembras de pulpa ardiente.

Cierro, cierro los labios, pero en rosas tremantes
se desata mi voz, como el agua en la fuente.

Que si no son pomposas, que si no son fragantes,
son las primeras rosas—hermano caminante—
de mi desconsolado jardín adolescente.

BEGINNING

Emerging under Helios, who sees me bleed,
I labor silently in my absent gardens.

My voice will be that of the sower of seed who sings
as he casts, among the sowed furrows of burning pulp.

I close, close my lips, but in trembling roses
my voice breaks loose, like water in the fountain.

If they're not pompous, if they're not fragrant,
they're the first roses—fellow traveler—
of my inconsolable adolescent garden.

Esta iglesia no tiene lampadarios votivos,
no tiene candelabros ni ceras amarillas,
no necesita el alma de vitrales ojivos
para besar las hostias y rezar de rodillas.

El sermón sin inciensos es como una semilla
de carne y luz que cae temblando al surco vivo:
el Padre-Nuestro, rezo de la vida sencilla,
tiene un sabor de pan frutal y primitivo...

Tiene un sabor de pan. Oloroso pan prieto
que allá en la infancia blanca entregó su secreto
a toda alma fragante que lo quiso escuchar...

Y el Padre-Nuestro en medio de la noche se pierde,
corre desnudo sobre las heredades verdes
y todo estremecido se sumerge en el mar...

This Church Does Not Have

This church does not have rows of votives,
does not have candelabra, nor yellow candles,
does not need the soul of stained-glass windows
to kiss the Communion wafer and pray on knees.

The sermon without incense is like a seed
of flesh and light that falls, trembling, to the living furrow:
the Our Father, prayer for the modest life,
has the flavor of fruit bread, of the primitive...

has the flavor of bread. Dark, sweet-smelling bread
that upon my white childhood delivered its secret
to every fragrant soul that wanted to hear it.

And in the middle of the night the Our Father loses its way,
runs naked across the green country estates
and, shaken, submerges itself in the sea...

PANTHEOS

Oh pedazo, pedazo de miseria, en qué vida
tienes tus manos albas y tu cabeza triste?
...Y tanto andar, y tanto llorar las cosas idas
sin saber qué dolores fueron los que tuviste.

Sin saber qué pan blanco te nutrió, ni qué duna
te envolvió con su arena, te fundió en su calor,
sin saber si eres carne, si eres sol, si eres luna,
sin saber si sufriste nuestro mismo dolor.

Si estás en este árbol o si lloras conmigo,
qué es lo que quieres, pedazo de miseria y amigo
de la cansada carne que no quiere perderte?

Si quieres no nos digas de qué racimo somos,
no nos digas el cuándo, no nos digas el cómo,
pero dinos adónde nos llevará la muerte...

PANTHEOS

O shard, shard of misery, in what life
do you have your white hands and your sad head?
...And so much walking, and so much weeping for things long gone,
without knowing which pains were yours.

Without knowing what white bread sustained you, or which dune
wrapped you in its sand, cast you with its heat,
without knowing if you are flesh, if you are sun, if you are moon,
without knowing if you suffered our same pain.

If you are in this tree or if you weep with me,
what is it you want, shard of misery and friend,
from the tired flesh that does not want to lose you?

If you don't want to tell us from what cluster we come
not tell us when, not tell us how,
tell us where death will take us...

Viejo ciego, llorabas

Viejo ciego, llorabas cuando tu vida era
buena, cuando tenías en tus ojos el sol:
pero si ya el silencio llegó, qué es lo que esperas,
qué es lo que esperas, ciego, qué esperas del dolor?

En tu rincón semejas un niño que naciera
sin pies para la tierra, sin ojos para el mar
y que como las bestias entre la noche ciega
—sin día y sin crepúsculo—se cansan de esperar.

Porque si tú conoces el camino que lleva
en dos o tres minutos hacia la vida nueva,
viejo ciego, qué esperas, qué puedes esperar?

Y si por la amargura más bruta del destino,
animal viejo y ciego, no sabes el camino,
ya que tengo dos ojos te lo puedo enseñar.

OLD MAN, YOU CRIED

Blind old man, you cried when your life was
good, when your eyes held the sun,
but if the silence has already arrived, for what are you waiting,
for what are you waiting, blind old man, are you waiting for
      the pain?

In your corner you resemble a boy who was born
without feet fit for the earth, without eyes for the sea
and who is like the beasts that in the blind night
—with no daylight and no twilight—grow tired of waiting.

For if you know the path that arrives
in two or three minutes at a new life,
blind old man, what are you waiting for, for what could you
      be waiting?

And if because of the most brutal bitterness of your destiny,
blind old animal, you do not know the path,
I, who have two eyes, can show it to you.

El nuevo soneto a Helena

Cuando estés vieja, niña (Ronsard ya te lo dijo),
te acordarás de aquellos versos que yo decía.
Tendrás los senos tristes de amamantar tus hijos,
los últimos retoños de tu vida vacía...

Yo estaré tan lejano que tus manos de cera
ararán el recuerdo de mis ruinas desnudas,
comprenderás que puede nevar en Primavera
y que en la Primavera las nieves son más crudas.

Yo estaré tan lejano que el amor y la pena
que antes vacié en la vida como un ánfora plena
estarán condenados a morir en mis manos...

Y será tarde porque se fue mi adolescencia,
tarde porque las flores una vez dan esencia
y porque aunque me llames yo estaré tan lejano.

New Sonnet for Helen

When you grow old, young girl (as Ronsard already told you),
you'll recall those verses I recited.
You'll have sad breasts from suckling your children,
the last buds of your empty life…

I'll be so far away that your hands of wax
will plow the memory of my naked ruins,
you'll understand it can snow in spring
and in spring the snows are harsher.

I'll be so far away the love and the grief
I earlier emptied into your life as in a full amphora
will be condemned to die in my hands…

And it will be late because my adolescence departed,
late because only once do flowers give off their essence
and because, though you call to me, I will be far away.

SENSACIÓN DE DOLOR

Fragancia
de lilas…

Claros atardeceres de mi lejana infancia
que fluyó como el cauce de unas aguas tranquilas.

Y después un pañuelo temblando en la distancia.
Bajo el cielo de seda la estrella que titila.

Nada más. Pies cansados en las largas errancias
y un dolor, un dolor que remuerde y se afila.

…Y a lo lejos campanas, canciones, penas, ansias,
vírgenes que tenían tan dulces las pupilas.

Fragancia
de lilas…

SENSE OF SMELL

Scent
of lilacs...

Clear twilights of my distant childhood
that flowed like the channel of some tranquil waters.

And later a handkerchief trembling in the distance.
Under the silken sky, the star that flickers.

Nothing more. Weary feet on long wanderings
and a pain, a pain that gnaws and sharpens itself.

...And in the distance bells, songs, sorrows, anguish,
virgins that had such sweet pupils.

Scent
of lilacs...

IVRESSE

Hoy que danza en mi cuerpo la pasión de Paolo
y ebrio de un sueño alegre mi corazón se agita:
hoy que sé la alegría de ser libre y ser solo
como el pistilo de una margarita infinita:

oh mujer—carne y sueño—, ven a encantarme un poco,
ven a vaciar tus copas de sol en mi camino:
que en mi barco amarillo tiemblen tus senos locos
y ebrios de juventud, que es el más bello vino.

Es bello porque nosotros lo bebemos
en estos temblorosos vasos de nuestro ser
que nos niegan el goce para que lo gocemos.
Bebamos.
Nunca dejemos de beber.

Nunca, mujer, rayo de luz, pulpa blanca de poma;
suavices la pisada que no te hará sufrir.
Sembremos la llanura antes de arar la loma.
Vivir será primero, después será morir.

Y después que en la ruta se apaguen nuestras huellas
y en el azul paremos nuestras blancas escalas
—flechas de oro que atajan en vano las estrellas—,
oh Francesca, hacia dónde te llevarán mis alas!

IVRESSE

Today the passion of Paul dances in my body
and drunk on a joyful dream my heart shudders:
Today I know the joy of being free and being alone
like the pistil of an infinite daisy:

O woman—flesh and dream—come enchant me a little,
come empty your cups of sun on my road:
in my yellow ship your breasts shake crazy
and drunk with youth, which is the most beautiful wine.

It is beautiful because we drink it
in these shaking glasses of our being
which deny us our joy so we can enjoy it.
Let us drink.
Let us never stop drinking.

Never, woman, ray of light, white apple pulp,
soften the footstep that will not bring suffering.
Let us sow the plain before plowing the hillock.
First will be the living, later will be the dying.

And later along the route, our footprints dim
and in the blue we raise our white ladders
—arrows of gold that in vain trap the stars—
O Francesca, where will my wings take you!

Cabellera rubia, suelta,
corriendo como un estero,
cabellera.

Uñas duras y doradas,
flores curvas y sensuales,
uñas duras y doradas.

Comba del vientre, escondida,
y abierta como una fruta
o una herida.

Dulce rodilla desnuda
apretada en mis rodillas,
dulce rodilla desnuda.

Enredadera del pelo
entre la oferta redonda
de los senos.

Huella que dura en el lecho,
huella dormida en el alma,
palabras locas.

Perdidas palabras locas:
rematarán mis canciones,
se morirán nuestras bocas.

Morena, la Besadora,
rosal de todas las rosas
en una hora.

MORENA, SHE WHO KISSES

Blond hair, loose,
flowing like a palm mat,
her head of hair.

Nails hard and golden,
flowers, curved and sensual,
nails hard and golden.

Curve of the belly, hidden,
and open like a fruit
or a wound.

Sweet naked knee
squeezed between my knees,
sweet naked knee.

Ivy of hair
between the round offer
of the breasts.

Lasting footprint in the bed,
footprint asleep in the soul,
crazy words.

Lost crazy words:
my songs will end,
our mouths will die.

The brown girl, the kisser,
rosebush of every rose
in one hour.

Besadora, dulce y rubia,
me iré,
te irás, Besadora.

Pero aún tengo la aurora
enredada en cada sien.

Bésame, por eso, ahora,
bésame, Besadora,
ahora y en la hora
de nuestra muerte.

                    Amén.

Kisser, sweet and blond,
I'll leave,
you'll leave, you who kiss.

But still I have the dawn
tangled up in each temple.

For that, kiss me now,
kiss me, Kisser,
now and at the hour
of your death.

Amen.

ORACIÓN

Carne doliente y machacada,
raudal de llanto sobre cada
noche de jergón malsano:
en esta hora yo quisiera
ver encantarse mis quimeras
a flor de labio, pecho y mano,
para que desciendan ellas
—las puras y únicas estrellas
de los jardines de mi amor—
en caravanas impolutas
sobre las almas de las putas
de estas ciudades del dolor.

Mal de amor, sensual laceria:
campana negra de miseria:
rosas del lecho de arrabal,
abierto al mal como un camino
por donde va el placer y el vino
desde la gloria al hospital.

En esta hora en que las lilas
sacuden sus hojas tranquilas
para botar el polvo impuro,
vuela mi espíritu intocado,
traspasa el huerto y el vallado,
abre la puerta, salta el muro

y va enredando en su camino
el mal dolor, el agrio sino
y desnudando la raigambre
de las mujeres que lucharon

PRAYER

Flesh aching and pounded,
torrent of weeping over each
night of sick straw mattress:
in this hour I would want
to see my chimeras cast a spell
on the tip of tongue, chest and hand,
so that they descend
—the pure and only stars
of the gardens of my love—
in immaculate caravans
over the souls of the whores
of these cities of pain.

Ill of love, sensual poverty:
black bell of misery:
roses of the suburban bed
open to evil like a path
where the pleasure and the wine pass
from the glory to the hospital.

In this hour in which the lilacs
calmly shake their leaves
to cast off the impure dust,
my untouched spirit flies,
passes the orchard and the fence,
opens the door, jumps the wall

and goes tangling up on its way
the sick pain, the bitter fate,
and undressing the roots
of the women who fought

y cayeron
y pecaron
y murieron
bajo los látigos del hambre.

No sólo es seda lo que escribo:
que el verso mío sea vivo
como recuerdo en tierra ajena
para alumbrar la mala suerte
de los que van hacia la muerte
como la sangre por las venas.

De los que van desde la vida
rotas las manos doloridas
en todas las zarzas ajenas:
de los que en estas horas quietas
no tienen madres ni poetas
para la pena.

Porque la frente en esta hora
se dobla y la mirada llora
saltando dolores y muros:
en esta hora en que las lilas
sacuden sus hojas tranquilas
para botar el polvo impuro.

and fell
and sinned
and died
under the whips of hunger.

Silk alone is not what I write:
may my verse be alive
like memory on foreign land
to shine light on the bad luck
of those moving toward death
like blood through the veins.

Of those who go through life
their aching hands broken
in foreign blackberry bushes:
of those who in these still hours
have neither mothers nor poets
for suffering.

Because in this hour the brow
folds and the visage weeps
leaping over pains and walls:
in this hour in which the lilacs
calmly shake their leaves
to cast off the impure dust.

El estribillo del turco

Flor el pantano vertiente la roca:
tu alma embellece lo que toca.

La carne pasa, tu vida queda
toda en mi verso de sangre o de seda.

Hay que ser dulce sobre todas las cosas:
más que un chacal vale una mariposa.

Eres gusano que labra y opera:
para ti crecen las verdes moreras.

Para que tejas tu seda celeste
la ciudad parece tranquila y agreste.

Gusano que labras, de pronto eres viejo:
el dolor del mundo crispa tus artejos!

A la muerte tu alma desnuda se asoma,
y le brotan alas de águila y paloma!

Y guarda la tierra tus vírgenes actas
hermano gusano, tus sedas intactas.

Vive en el alba y el crepúsculo,
adora el tigre y el corpúsculo,
comprende la polea y el músculo!

Que se te vaya la vida, hermano,
no en lo divino sino en lo humano,
no en las estrellas sino en tus manos.

THE REFRAIN OF THE TURK

Flower of marsh pouring over the rock:
your soul makes beautiful what it touches.

The flesh dries, your life remains
all in my verse of blood or of silk.

One needs to be kind above all else:
a butterfly is worth more than a jackal.

You are worm that labors and produces:
for you the green mulberries grow.

So that you sow your celestial silk
the city appears calm and rural.

Worm that labors, suddenly you are old:
the pain of the world contorts your knuckles!

Your naked soul sticks out its head to glance at death,
and sprouts wings of eagle and dove!

And the earth keeps your virgin accords
brother worm, your intact silks.

You live in the dawn and the dusk,
adore the tiger and the corpuscle,
understand the pulley and the muscle!

Let life take its leave of you, brother,
not in the divine but in the human,
not in the stars but in your hands.

Que llegará la noche y luego
serás de tierra, de viento o de fuego.

Por eso deja que todas tus puertas
se cimbren, a todos los vientos abiertas.

Y de tu huerta al viajero convida:
dale al viajero la flor de tu vida!

Y no seas duro, ni parco, ni terco,
sé una frutaleda sin garfios ni cercos!

Dulce hay que ser y darse a todos,
para vivir no hay otro modo

de ser dulces. Darse a las gentes
como a la tierra las vertientes.

Y no temer. Y no pensar.
Dar para volver a dar.

Que quien se da no se termina
porque hay en él pulpa divina.

Cómo se dan sin terminarse, hermano mío,
al mar las aguas de los ríos!

Que mi canto en tu vida dore lo que deseas.
Tu buena voluntad torne en luz lo que miras.
Que tu vida así sea.

—Mentira, mentira, mentira!

Night will arrive and then
you'll be of earth, of wind and of fire.

For that, let all your doors
shake, open to every wind.

And to your orchard invite the traveler:
give the traveler the flower of your life!

And don't be hard, or cheap, or stubborn,
be a grove of fruit trees without hooks or fences!

One must be kind and give oneself to everyone,
there is no other way to live

but to be sweet. Give yourself to people
as do mountain slopes to the earth.

Don't be afraid. Don't think.
Give to give again.

Who gives of himself never ends
because in him is the pulp of the divine.

Like the waters of the rivers give themselves
to the sea, my brother, without end!

May my song in your life gild what you desire.
May your goodwill turn into light what you see.
May your life be as such.

—Lies, lies, lies!

El castillo maldito

Mientras camino, la acera va golpeándome los pies,
el fulgor de las estrellas me va rompiendo los ojos.
Se me cae un pensamiento como se cae una mies
del carro que tambaleando raya los pardos rastrojos.

Oh pensamientos perdidos que nunca nadie recoge,
si la palabra se dice, la sensación queda adentro:
espiga sin madurar, Satanás le encuentre troje
que yo con los ojos rotos no le busco ni le encuentro!

Que yo con los ojos rotos sigo una ruta sin fin...
Por qué de los pensamientos, por qué de la vida en vano?
Como se muere la música si se deshace el violín,
no moveré mi canción cuando no mueva mis manos.

Alto de mi corazón en la explanada desierta
donde estoy crucificado como el dolor en un verso...
Mi vida es un gran castillo sin ventanas y sin puertas
y para que tú no llegues por esta senda,
                                      la tuerzo.

The Cursed Castle

While I walk, the sidewalk goes on pounding my feet,
the shine of the stars goes on shattering my eyes.
A thought falls from me as falls an ear of grain
from the cart that, staggering, carves lines in the brown stubble.

O lost thoughts that no one ever gathers up,
if the word is spoken, the sensation remains within:
unripened sprig, may Satan find the granary
that I with broken eyes neither seek nor find!

That I, with eyes broken, follow a route without end...
Why thoughts, why life in vain?
Just as the music dies when the violin comes undone,
I will not move my song if I don't move my hands.

Height of my heart in the deserted esplanade
where I am crucified like pain in a line of verse.
My life is a great castle without windows and without doors
and so that you don't arrive by this pathway,

I twist it.

FAREWELL, Y LOS SOLLOZOS

FAREWELL, AND THE SOBBING

Farewell

Desde el fondo de ti, y arrodillado,
un niño triste, como yo, nos mira.

Por esa vida que arderá en sus venas
tendrían que amarrarse nuestras vidas.

Por esas manos, hijas de tus manos,
tendrían que matar las manos mías.

Por sus ojos abiertos en la tierra
veré en los tuyos lágrimas un día.

2

Yo no lo quiero, Amada.

Para que nada nos amarre
que no nos una nada.

Ni la palabra que aromó tu boca,
ni lo que no dijeron las palabras.

Ni la fiesta de amor que no tuvimos,
ni tus sollozos junto a la ventana.

3

(Amo el amor de los marineros
que besan y se van.

FAREWELL

From the depth of you, and kneeling,
a sad boy, like me, watches us.

For that life that will burn in his veins
our lives would have to bind together.

For those hands, daughters of your hands,
these hands of mine would have to kill.

Through his eyes open on the earth
I someday will see, in your eyes, tears.

2

That, my Beloved, I don't want.

So that nothing binds us
nothing brings us together.

Not the word that scented your mouth,
nor what the words did not say.

Not the feast of love we did not share,
or your sobbing by the window.

3

(I love the love of the sailors
who kiss and leave.

Dejan una promesa.
No vuelven nunca más.

En cada puerto una mujer espera:
los marineros besan y se van.

Una noche se acuestan con la muerte
en el lecho del mar.

4

Amo el amor que se reparte
en besos, lecho y pan.

Amor que puede ser eterno
y puede ser fugaz.

Amor que quiere libertarse
para volver a amar.

Amor divinizado que se acerca.
Amor divinizado que se va.)

5

Ya no se encantarán mis ojos en tus ojos,
ya no se endulzará junto a ti mi dolor.

Pero hacia donde vaya llevaré tu mirada
y hacia donde camines llevarás mi dolor.

Fui tuyo, fuiste mía. Qué más? Juntos hicimos
un recodo en la ruta donde el amor pasó.

They leave a promise.
They never return.

In every port a woman waits:
the sailors kiss and go away.

A night lies down with death
in the bed of the sea.

4

I love the love that spreads
in kisses, bed and bread.

Love that can be eternal
and can be fleeting.

Love that wants to be free
to love again.

Godly love that approaches.
Godly love that leaves.)

5

No longer will my eyes savor your eyes,
no longer will my pain grow sweeter beside you.

But wherever I go I will take your gaze,
wherever you walk you will take my pain.

I was yours, you were mine. What more? Together we took
a bend in the road where the love happened.

Fui tuyo, fuiste mía. Tú serás del que te ame,
del que corte en tu huerto lo que he sembrado yo.

Yo me voy. Estoy triste: pero siempre estoy triste.
Vengo desde tus brazos. No sé hacia dónde voy.

...Desde tu corazón me dice adiós un niño.
Y yo le digo adiós.

I was yours, you were mine. You'll be of him who loves you,
who cuts in your garden what I have sown.

I leave. I am sad: but I'm always sad.
I come from your arms. I don't know where I go.

...From your heart a boy says goodbye to me.
And I say goodbye to him.

El padre

Tierra de sembradura inculta y brava,
tierra en que no hay esteros ni caminos,
mi vida bajo el Sol tiembla y se alarga.

Padre, tus ojos dulces nada pueden,
como nada pudieron las estrellas
que me abrasan los ojos y las sienes.

El mal de amor me enceguéció la vista
y en la fontana dulce de mi sueño
se reflejó otra fuente estremecida.

Después... Pregunta a Dios por qué me dieron
lo que me dieron y por qué después
supe una soledad de tierra y cielo.

Mira, mi juventud fue un brote puro
que se quedó sin estallar y pierde
su dulzura de sangres y de jugos.

El sol que cae y cae eternamente
se cansó de besarla... Y el otoño.
Padre, tus ojos dulces nada pueden.

Escucharé en la noche tus palabras:
        ...niño, mi niño...
                        Y en la noche inmensa
seguiré con mis llagas y tus llagas.

THE FATHER

Land of uncultivated and brave sowing,
land in which are neither marshes nor roads,
my life under the Sun shudders and grows longer.

Father, your kind eyes can do nothing,
like nothing the stars—which burn my eyes
and my temples—were able to do.

The malevolence of love blinded me
and in the sweet fountain of my dream
was reflected another trembling spring.

Later... Ask God why they gave me
what they gave me and why later
I knew a solitude of land and sky.

Look, my youth was a pure sprout
that never burst and now it loses
its sweetness of bloods and juices.

The sun that eternally falls and falls
grew tired of kissing her... And autumn.
Father, your kind eyes can do nothing.

At night I will listen to your words:
          ...child, my child...
                              And in the immense night
I will go on with my wounds and your sores.

El ciego de la pandereta

Ciego, siempre será tu ayer mañana?
Siempre estará tu pandereta pobre
estremeciendo tus manos crispadas?

Yo voy pasando y veo tu silueta
y me parece que es tu corazón
el que se cimbra con tu pandereta.

Yo pasé ayer y supe tu dolor:
dolor que siendo yo quien lo ha sabido
es mucho mayor.

No volveré por no volverte a ver,
pero mañana tu silueta negra
estará como ayer:
la mano que recibe
los ojos que no ven,
la cara parda, lastimosa y triste,
golpeando en cada salto la pared.

Ciego, ya voy pasando y ya te miro,
y de rabia y dolor—qué sé yo qué—
algo me aprieta el corazón,
el corazón y la sien.

Por tus ojos que nunca han mirado
cambiara yo los míos que te ven!

The Blind Man with Tambourine

Blind man, will your yesterday always be tomorrow?
Will your poor tambourine always be
shaking your contorted hands?

I'm passing by and see your silhouette
and it seems that it's your heart
that quivers with your tambourine.

I passed by yesterday and I knew your pain:
pain which for being me who has known it
is much greater.

I will not return, not see you again,
but tomorrow your black silhouette
will be as it was yesterday:
the hand that reached out,
the eyes that cannot see,
the brown face, pitiful and sad,
with each leap striking the wall.

Blind man, now I'm passing by and now I see you,
and from rage and pain—what do I know!—
something presses on my heart,
my heart and my temple.

For your eyes which have never seen you
I'd exchange mine which do!

Amor

Mujer, yo hubiera sido tu hijo, por beberte
la leche de los senos como de un manantial,
por mirarte y sentirte a mi lado y tenerte
en la risa de oro y la voz de cristal.

Por sentirte en mis venas como Dios en los ríos
y adorarte en los tristes huesos de polvo y cal,
porque tu ser pasara sin pena al lado mío
y saliera en la estrofa—limpio de todo mal—.

Cómo sabría amarte, mujer, cómo sabría
amarte, amarte como nadie supo jamás!
Morir y todavía
amarte más.
Y todavía
amarte más
            y más.

LOVE

Woman, I'd have liked to have been your son, to drink
the milk from your breasts as from a spring,
to see and feel you by my side and have you
in the laughter of gold and the voice of crystal.

To feel you in my veins like God in the rivers
and to adore you in the sad bones of dust and lime,
because your being will pass without shame beside me
and would take leave in the stanza—cleansed of all evil—.

How would I know to love you, woman, how would I know
to love you, love you as no one else knew how.
To die and still
love you more.
And still
love you more
                    and more.

Se va la poesía de las cosas
o no la puede condensar mi vida?
Ayer—mirando el último crepúsculo—
yo era un manchón de musgo entre unas ruinas.

Las ciudades—hollines y venganzas—,
la cochinada gris de los suburbios,
la oficina que encorva las espaldas,
el jefe de ojos turbios.

Sangre de un arrebol sobre los cerros,
sangre sobre las calles y las plazas,
dolor de corazones rotos,
podre de hastíos y de lágrimas.

Un río abraza el arrabal como una
mano helada que tienta en las tinieblas:
sobre sus aguas
se avergüenzan de verse las estrellas.

Y las casas que esconden los deseos
detrás de las ventanas luminosas,
mientras afuera el viento
lleva un poco de barro a cada rosa.

Lejos... la bruma de las olvidanzas
—humos espesos, tajamares rotos—
y el campo, el campo verde! en que jadean
los bueyes y los hombres sudorosos.

NEIGHBORHOOD WITHOUT LIGHT

Does poetry depart from things
or is my life not able to distill it?
Yesterday—watching the last of twilight—
I was a patch of moss among some ruins.

The cities—soot and vengeance—,
the gray filth of the suburbs,
the office that bends backs,
the boss with roiled eyes.

Blood of a red glow over the hills,
blood in the streets and the plazas,
ache of broken hearts,
rot of disgust and of tears.

A river embraces the outskirts of the city like a
frozen hand that feels its way in the darkness:
above its waters
the stars are ashamed to be seen.

And the houses that hide desires
behind lit windows
while outside the wind
brings a little mud to each rose.

Far away… the mist of forgetfulness
—thick smoke, broken edge of dikes—
and the country, the green country! in which pant
the oxen and the sweating men.

Y aquí estoy yo, brotado entre las ruinas,
mordiendo solo todas las tristezas,
como si el llanto fuera una semilla
y yo el único surco de la tierra.

And here I am; sprouted among the ruins,
alone, chewing on all the sadness,
as if the weeping were a seed
and I the only furrow on the earth.

PUENTES

Puentes: arcos de acero azul adonde vienen
a dar su despedida los que pasan,
—por arriba los trenes,
por abajo las aguas—,
enfermos de seguir un largo viaje
que principia, que sigue y nunca acaba.
Cielos—arriba—, cielos,
y pájaros que pasan
sin detenerse, caminando como
los trenes y las aguas.

Qué maldición cayó sobre vosotros?
Qué esperáis en la noche densa y larga
con los brazos abiertos como un niño
que muere a la llegada de su hermana?

Qué voz de maldición pasiva y negra
sobre vosotros extendió sus alas,
para hacer que siguieran
el viaje que no acaba
los paisajes, la vida, el sol, la tierra,
los trenes y las aguas,
mientras la angustia inmóvil del acero
se hunde más en la tierra y más la clava?

BRIDGES

Bridges: arches of blue steel where the ones
who pass come to say their farewell,
—above, the trains,
below, the waters—
sick from following on a long journey
that begins, goes on, and never ends.
Skies—above—skies,
and birds that pass by
without stopping, making their way like
the trains and the waters.

What curse came over you?
For what do you wait in the long and dense night
with open arms like a child
who dies upon the arrival of his sister?

What voice of an inert and black curse
spread its wings over you,
to make sure the landscapes, life, sun, earth,
the trains, and the waters continue
the journey that does not end
while the motionless anguish of the steel
sinks deeper into the earth, and drives the nail deeper?

MAESTRANZAS DE NOCHE

Fierro negro que duerme, fierro negro que gime
por cada poro un grito de desconsolación.

Las cenizas ardidas sobre la tierra triste,
los caldos en que el bronce derritió su dolor.

Aves de qué lejano país desventurado
graznaron en la noche dolorosa y sin fin?

Y el grito se me crispa como un nervio enroscado
o como la cuerda rota de un violín.

Cada máquina tiene una pupila abierta
para mirarme a mí.

En las paredes cuelgan las interrogaciones,
florece en las bigornias el alma de los bronces
y hay un temblor de pasos en los cuartos desiertos.

Y entre la noche negra—desesperadas—corren
y sollozan las almas de los obreros muertos.

NIGHT ARMORY

Black iron that sleeps, black iron that groans
from every pore, a shout of grief.

The burnt ashes over the sad land,
the broths in which the bronze melted its pain.

Birds from what unfortunate, faraway country
cawed in the painful night with no end?

And the shriek made me stiffen like a coiled nerve
or like the broken string of a violin.

Each machine keeps a pupil open
looking at me.

On the walls hang the questions,
the soul of the bronzes blooms in the double-beaked anvil
and there is a tremor of footsteps in the deserted rooms.

And in the black night—desperate—run
and sob the souls of the dead workers.

La pata gris del Malo pisó estas pardas tierras,
hirió estos dulces surcos, movió estos curvos montes,
rasguñó las llanuras guardadas por la hilera
rural de las derechas alamedas bifrontes.

El terraplén yacente removió su cansancio,
se abrió como una mano desesperada el cerro,
en cabalgatas ebrias galopaban las nubes
arrancando de Dios, de la tierra y del cielo.

El agua entró en la tierra mientras la tierra huía
abiertas las entrañas y anegada la frente:
hacia los cuatro vientos, en las tardes malditas,
rodaban—ululando como tigres—los trenes.

Yo soy una palabra de este paisaje muerto,
yo soy el corazón de este cielo vacío:
cuando voy por los campos, con el alma en el viento,
mis venas continúan el rumor de los ríos.

A dónde vas ahora?—Sobre el cielo la greda
del crepúsculo, para los dedos de la noche.
No alumbrarán estrellas... A mis ojos se enredan
aromos rubios en los campos de Loncoche.

BLOND ACACIAS IN THE FIELDS OF LONCOCHE

The gray paw of the Evil One strode across these brown lands,
wounded these sweet furrows, moved these curved mountains,
scratched the plains guarded by the rural rows
of straight poplars, each facing the other.

The reclining slope removed its exhaustion,
the hill opened like a desperate hand,
in drunk processions the clouds galloped
tearing away from God, from the earth and the sky.

The water entered the earth as the earth was fleeing,
the bowels open and the brow flooded:
toward the four winds, in the cursed afternoons,
the trains—howling like tigers—rolled.

I am one word of this dead landscape,
I am the heart of this empty sky:
when I pass through the fields, with my soul in the wind,
my veins carry on with the rumor of the rivers.

Where're you going now?—Upon the sky the sandy clay
of twilight, for the fingers of the night.
The stars will not illuminate... In my eyes blond acacias
are woven together in the fields of Loncoche.

GRITA

Amor, llegado que hayas a mi fuente lejana,
cuida de no morderme con tu voz de ilusión:
que mi dolor oscuro no se muera en tus alas,
que en tu garganta de oro no se ahogue mi voz.

Amor—llegado que hayas
a mi fuente lejana,
sé turbión que desuella
sé rompiente que clava.

Amor, deshace el ritmo
de mis aguas tranquilas:
sabe ser el dolor que retiembla y que sufre,
sábeme ser la angustia que se retuerce y grita.

No me des el olvido.
No me des la ilusión.
Porque todas las hojas que a la tierra han caído
me tienen amarillo de oro el corazón.

Amor—llegado que hayas
a mi fuente lejana,
tuérceme las vertientes,
críspame las entrañas.
Y así una tarde—Amor de manos crueles—,
arrodillado, te daré las gracias.

CRY OUT

Love, arrival that finds my fountain far away,
take care not to bite me with your illusory voice:
that my dark pain does not die in your wings,
that in your golden throat my voice not drown.

Love—arrival that finds
my fountain far away,
be downpour that flays
be breaking that drives nails.

Love, the rhythm
of my tranquil waters dissolves:
knows how to be the pain that shudders and suffers,
knows me to be the anguish that writhes and cries out.

Do not give me oblivion.
Do not give me illusion.
Because all the leaves that have fallen to the earth
turn my heart yellow with gold.

Love—arrival that finds
my fountain far away,
entwine my slopes,
contort my entrails.
And, like that, one afternoon—Love of cruel hands—
on my knees, I will thank you.

LOS JUGADORES

Juegan, juegan.
Agachados, arrugados, decrépitos.

Este hombre torvo
junto a los mares de su patria, más lejana que el sol,
cantó bellas canciones.

Canción de la belleza de la tierra,
canción de la belleza de la Amada,
canción, canción
que no precisa fin.

Este otro de la mano en la frente,
pálido como la última hoja de un árbol,
debe tener hijas rubias
de carne apretada,
granada,
rosada.

Juegan, juegan.

Los miro entre la vaga bruma del gas y el humo.
Y mirando estos hombres sé que la vida es triste.

THE GAMBLERS

They play, play.
Hunched over, wrinkled, decrepit.

This man, terrifying,
beside the seas of his motherland, farther than the sun,
sang beautiful songs.

Song of the beauty of the land,
song of the beauty of the Beloved,
song, song
that states no end.

This one with hand on forehead,
pale as the last leaf of a tree,
must have blond daughters
with firm flesh,
ripe,
pink.

They gamble, gamble.

I see them through the vague haze of gas and smoke.
And watching these men I know life is sad.

LOS CREPÚSCULOS DE MARURI

THE TWILIGHTS OF MARURI

LA TARDE SOBRE LOS TEJADOS

(Lentísimo)

La tarde sobre los tejados
cae
y cae...
Quién le dio para que viniera
alas de ave?

Y este silencio que lo llena
      todo,
desde qué país de astros
      se vino solo?

Y por qué esta bruma
      —plúmula trémula—
beso de lluvia
      —sensitiva—

cayó en silencio—y para siempre—
      sobre mi vida?

EVENING OVER THE TILE ROOFS

(lentissimo)

Evening over the tile roofs
falls
and falls...
Who gave it, so it would come,
bird wings?

And this silence that fills
     everything,
from what country of stars
     did it come alone?

And why did this mist
     —trembling bud—
kiss of rain
     —sensitive—

fall in silence—and forever—
     over my life?

SI DIOS ESTÁ EN MI VERSO

Perro mío,
si Dios está en mi verso,
Dios soy yo.
Si Dios está en tus ojos doloridos,
tú eres Dios.

Y en este mundo inmenso nadie existe
que se arrodille ante nosotros dos!

If God Is in My Verse

Dog of mine,
if God is in my verse,
God is me.
If God is in your sorrowful eyes,
you are God.

And in this immense world no one exists
who will kneel before us.

Amigo

1

Amigo, llévate lo que tú quieras,
penetra tu mirada en los rincones,
y si así lo deseas, yo te doy mi alma entera,
con sus blancas avenidas y sus canciones.

2

Amigo—con la tarde haz que se vaya
este inútil y viejo deseo de vencer.
Bebe en mi cántaro si tienes sed.
Amigo—con la tarde haz que se vaya
este deseo mío de que todo rosal
me pertenezca.

Amigo,
si tienes hambre come de mi pan.

3

Todo, amigo, lo he hecho para ti. Todo esto
que sin mirar verás en mi estancia desnuda:
todo esto que se eleva por los muros derechos
—como mi corazón—siempre buscando altura.

Te sonríes—amigo. Qué importa! Nadie sabe
entregar en las manos lo que se esconde adentro,
pero yo te doy mi alma, ánfora de mieles suaves,
y todo te lo doy... Menos aquel recuerdo...

FRIEND

1

Friend, take whatever you want,
penetrate with your gaze the corners,
and if you so desire, I'll give you my entire soul,
with its white avenues and its songs.

2

Friend—with the evening, make
this old and useless desire to win go away.
Drink of my clay pitcher if you are thirsty.
Friend—with the evening, make go away
this desire of mine that every rosebush
belong to me.

        Friend,
if you're hungry, eat of my bread.

3

Everything, friend, I have done for you. All this
that without looking you'll see in my naked room:
all this that ascends the straight walls
—like my heart—always seeking altitude.

You smile—friend. What does it matter! No one knows
how to deliver in the hands what's hidden inside,
but I give you my soul, amphora of soft honeys,
and I give everything to you... Less that one memory...

Que en mi heredad vacía aquel amor perdido
es una rosa blanca que se abre en silencio...

In my empty estate, that lost love
is a white rose that opens in silence...

MARIPOSA DE OTOÑO

La mariposa volotea
y arde—con el sol—a veces.

Mancha volante y llamarada,
ahora se queda parada
sobre una hoja que la mece.

Me decían: —No tienes nada.
No estás enfermo. Te parece.

Yo tampoco decía nada.
Y pasó el tiempo de las mieses.

Hoy una mano de congoja
llena de Otoño el horizonte.
Y hasta de mi alma caen hojas.

Me decían: —No tienes nada.
No estás enfermo. Te parece.

Era la hora de las espigas.
El sol, ahora,
convalece.

Todo se va en la vida, amigos.
Se va o perece.

Se va la mano que te induce.
Se va o perece.

AUTUMN BUTTERFLY

The butterfly whirls about
and burns—with the sun—at times.

Flying stain and blaze,
now she stands still
on a leaf that rocks her.

They'd say to me: You have nothing.
You aren't sick. It seems to you.

I wouldn't say anything, either.
And the harvest time passed.

Today a hand of grief
fills the horizon with autumn.
And even from my soul leaves fall.

They'd say to me: You have nothing.
You aren't sick. It seems to you.

It was the hour of ears of grain.
Now, the sun
convalesces.

Friends, everything departs in life.
Departs or perishes.

The hand that urges you departs.
Leaves or perishes.

Se va la rosa que desates.
También la boca que te bese.

El agua, la sombra y el vaso.
Se va o perece.

Pasó la hora de las espigas.
El sol, ahora, convalece.

Su lengua tibia me rodea.
También me dice: —Te parece.

La mariposa volotea,
revolotea,
y desaparece.

The rose that you unleash departs.
Also the mouth that kisses you.

The water, the shadow and the glass.
Departs or perishes.

The hour of ears of grain passed.
Now, the sun convalesces.

Its tepid tongue surrounds me.
It also says to me: —It seems to you.

The butterfly whirls,
circles around,
and disappears.

Dios—de dónde sacaste para encender el cielo
este maravilloso crepúsculo de cobre?
Por él supe llenarme de alegría de nuevo,
y la mala mirada supe tornarla noble.

Entre las llamaradas amarillas y verdes
se alumbró el lampadario de un sol desconocido
que rajó las azules llanuras del Oeste
y volcó en las montañas sus fuentes y sus ríos.

Dame la maga fiesta, Dios, déjala en mi vida,
dame los fuegos tuyos para alumbrar la tierra,
deja en mi corazón tu lámpara encendida
y yo seré el aceite de su lumbre suprema.

Y me iré por los campos en la noche estrellada
con los brazos abiertos y la frente desnuda,
cantando aires ingenuos con las mismas palabras
que en la noche se dicen los campos y la luna.

GIVE ME THE MAGICAL FEAST

God—from where did you draw to light the sky,
this wondrous crepuscule of copper?
Because of it, I knew again how to fill with joy
and turn my wicked look noble.

Among the yellow and green flares
was lit the candelabrum of an unknown sun
that sliced the blue plains of the west
and dropped on the mountains their fountains and rivers.

Give me the magical feast. God, leave it in my life,
give me those fires of yours to illuminate the land,
leave in my heart your burning lamp
and I'll be the oil of its supreme light.

And I'll pass through the fields in the starry night
with open arms and bare brow,
singing naive airs with the same words
in the night which the fields and the moon say to each other.

ME PEINA EL VIENTO LOS CABELLOS

Me peina el viento los cabellos
como una mano maternal:
abro la puerta del recuerdo
y el pensamiento se me va.

Son otras voces las que llevo,
es de otros labios mi cantar:
hasta mi gruta de recuerdos
tiene una extraña claridad!

Frutos de tierras extranjeras,
olas azules de otro mar,
amores de otros hombres, penas
que no me atrevo a recordar.

Y el viento, el viento que me peina
como una mano maternal!
Mi verdad se pierde en la noche:
no tengo noche ni verdad!

Tendido en medio del camino
deben pisarme para andar.

Pasan por mí sus corazones
ebrios de vino y de soñar.

Yo soy un puente inmóvil entre
tu corazón y la eternidad.

Si me muriera de repente
no dejaría de cantar!

The Wind Combs My Hair

The wind combs my hair
like a mother's hand:
I open the door of remembrance
and thought leaves me.

They are other voices I carry,
my singing comes from other lips:
until my grotto of memories
takes on a strange clarity!

Fruits of foreign lands,
blue waves of another sea,
loves of other men, shame
that I dare not recall.

And the wind, the wind that combs me
like a maternal hand!
My truth is lost in the night:
I have neither night nor truth!

I lie in the middle of the road,
others must step over me to walk.

Their hearts drunk with wine
and dreaming pass through me.

I am a motionless bridge between
your heart and eternity.

If suddenly I were to die
I would not stop singing!

SAUDADE

Saudade—Qué será?... yo no sé... lo he buscado
en unos diccionarios empolvados y antiguos
y en otros libros que no me han dado el significado
de esta dulce palabra de perfiles ambiguos.

Dicen que azules son las montañas como ella,
que en ella se obscurecen los amores lejanos,
y un noble y buen amigo mío (y de las estrellas)
la nombra en un temblor de trenzas y de manos.

Y hoy en Eça de Queiroz sin mirar la adivino,
su secreto se evade, su dulzura me obsede
como una mariposa de cuerpo extraño y fino
siempre lejos—tan lejos!—de mis tranquilas redes.

Saudade... Oiga, vecino, sabe el significado
de esta palabra blanca que como un pez se evade?
No... Y me tiembla en la boca su temblor delicado...
Saudade...

SAUDADE

Saudade—What can it be?... I don't know... I've
       looked for it
in some dusty and ancient dictionaries
and in other books that haven't yielded the meaning
of this sweet word of ambiguous profiles.

They say that like her the mountains are blue,
that in her darken the distant loves,
and a noble and good friend of mine (and of the stars)
names her in a trembling of braids and of hands.

And today in Eça de Queiroz, without seeing it, they
       discern it,
her secret eludes, her sweetness obsesses me
like a butterfly of strange and delicate body
always far—so far!—from my calm nets.

Saudade... Say, neighbor, do you know the meaning
of this white word that like a fish escapes?
No... Your subtle tremor trembles in my mouth...
Saudade...

No lo había mirado

No lo había mirado y nuestros pasos
sonaban juntos.

Nunca escuché su voz y mi voz iba
llenando el mundo.

Y hubo un día de sol y mi alegría
en mí no cupo.

Sentí la angustia de cargar la nueva
soledad del crepúsculo.

Lo sentí junto a mí, brazos ardiendo,
limpio, sangrante, puro.

Y mi dolor, bajo la noche negra
entró en su corazón.

Y vamos juntos.

I Had Not Seen It

I had not seen it and our steps
sounded together.

I never heard its voice and my voice was
filling the world.

And it was a sunny day and my joy
didn't fit within me.

I felt the anguish of carrying the new
solitude of the dusk.

I felt it next to me, burning arms,
clean, bleeding, pure.

And my pain, in the black night,
entered its heart.

And we go together.

MI ALMA

Mi alma es un carrousel vacío en el crepúsculo...

MY SOUL

My soul is an empty merry-go-round in the twilight...

AQUÍ ESTOY CON MI POBRE CUERPO

Aquí estoy con mi pobre cuerpo frente al crepúsculo
que entinta de oros rojos el cielo de la tarde:
mientras entre la niebla los árboles oscuros
se libertan y salen a danzar por las calles.

Yo no sé por qué estoy aquí, ni cuándo vine,
ni por qué la luz roja del sol lo llena todo;
me basta con sentir frente a mi cuerpo triste
la inmensidad de un cielo de luz teñido de oro,

la inmensa rojedad de un sol que ya no existe,
el inmenso cadáver de una tierra ya muerta,
y frente a las astrales luminarias que tiñen el cielo,
la inmensidad de mi alma bajo la tarde inmensa.

HERE I AM WITH MY POOR BODY

Here I am with my poor body facing the twilight
that dyes with golden reds the evening sky:
while amid the mist the dark trees
free themselves and leave to dance in the streets.

I don't know why I'm here, nor when I came
nor why the red light of the sun fills everything;
it's enough to feel my sad body facing
the immensity of a gold-tinted sky,

the immense redness of a sun that no longer exists,
the immense corpse of a land already dead,
and facing the astral lights that color the sky,
the immensity of my soul beneath the immense evening.

Hoy, que es el cumpleaños de mi hermana, no tengo
nada que darle, nada. No tengo nada, hermana.
Todo lo que poseo siempre lo llevo lejos.
A veces hasta mi alma me parece lejana.

Pobre como una hoja amarilla de otoño
y cantor como un hilo de agua sobre una huerta:
los dolores, tú sabes cómo me caen todos
como al camino caen todas las hojas muertas.

Mis alegrías nunca las sabrás, hermanita,
y mi dolor es ése, no te las puedo dar:
vinieron como pájaros a posarse en mi vida,
una palabra dura las haría volar.

Pienso que también ellas me dejarán un día,
que me quedaré solo, como nunca lo estuve.
Tú lo sabes, hermana, la soledad me lleva
hacia el fin de la tierra como el viento a las nubes!

Pero para qué es esto de pensamientos tristes!
A ti menos que a nadie debe afligir mi voz!
Después de todo nada de esto que digo existe.
No vayas a contárselo a mi madre, por Dios!

Uno no sabe cómo va hilvanando mentiras,
y uno dice por ellas, y ellas hablan por uno.
Piensa que tengo el alma toda llena de risas,
y no te engañarás, hermana, te lo juro.

Today, Which Is My Sister's Birthday

Today, which is my sister's birthday, I have
nothing to give her, nothing. Sister, I have nothing.
Everything I possess I always carry afar.
Sometimes even my soul seems distant.

Poor like a yellow autumn leaf
and singing like a thread of water in an orchard:
the sorrows, you know how they all fall on me
like all the dead leaves fall on the road.

You will never know my joys, little sister,
and that is my sorrow—I can't give them to you:
they arrived like birds to perch in my life,
one harsh word and they will fly away.

I also think they'll leave me one day,
I'll be alone, as I never was.
Sister, you know solitude takes me
to the end of the earth as the wind the clouds.

But why all these sad thoughts!
My voice should trouble you less than anyone!
After all, none of this I say exists.
For God's sake, don't go telling my mother about this!

We don't know how one goes piecing lies together,
one speaks through them, they speak for us.
Believe that my entire soul is full of laughter,
and you won't deceive yourself, sister, I swear to you.

Mujer, nada me has dado

Nada me has dado y para ti mi vida
deshoja su rosal de desconsuelo,
porque ves estas cosas que yo miro,
las mismas tierras y los mismos cielos,

porque la red de nervios y de venas
que sostiene tu ser y tu belleza
se debe estremecer al beso puro
del sol, del mismo sol que a mí me besa.

Mujer, nada me has dado y sin embargo
a través de tu ser siento las cosas:
estoy alegre de mirar la tierra
en que tu corazón tiembla y reposa.

Me limitan en vano mis sentidos
—dulces flores que se abren en el viento—
porque adivino el pájaro que pasa
y que mojó de azul tu sentimiento.

Y sin embargo no me has dado nada,
no se florecen para mí tus años,
la cascada de cobre de tu risa
no apagará la sed de mis rebaños.

Hostia que no probó tu boca fina,
amador del amado que te llame,
saldré al camino con mi amor al brazo
como un vaso de miel para el que ames.

WOMAN, YOU'VE GIVEN ME NOTHING

You've given me nothing and for you my life
sheds the petals of its rosebush of grief,
because you see these things I see,
the same lands and the same skies,

because the net of nerves and veins
that sustains your being and your beauty
must tremble at the pure kiss
of the sun, the same sun that kisses me.

Woman, you've given me nothing and even so
through your being I feel things:
I am happy to look at the earth
in which your heart trembles and rests.

In vain my senses limit me
—sweet flowers that open in the wind—
because I discern the bird that passes
and that'll dampen your feelings with blue.

Nevertheless, you've given me nothing,
your years don't bloom for me,
the cascade of copper that's your laughter
won't extinguish the thirst of my flocks.

Host that your fine mouth didn't taste,
lover of the beloved who will call you,
I'll leave along the road with my love on my arm
like a glass of honey for he whom you will love.

———

Ya ves, noche estrellada, canto y copa
en que bebes el agua que yo bebo,
vivo en tu vida, vives en mi vida,
nada me has dado y todo te lo debo.

Now you see, night with stars, song and cup
in which you drink the water I drink,
I live in your life, you live in my life,
you've given me nothing and I owe you everything.

TENGO MIEDO

Tengo miedo. La tarde es gris y la tristeza
del cielo se abre como una boca de muerto.
Tiene mi corazón un llanto de princesa
olvidada en el fondo de un palacio desierto.

Tengo miedo. Y me siento tan cansado y pequeño
que reflejo la tarde sin meditar en ella.
(En mi cabeza enferma no ha de caber un sueño
así como en el cielo no ha cabido una estrella.)

Sin embargo en mis ojos una pregunta existe
y hay un grito en mi boca que mi boca no grita.
No hay oído en la tierra que oiga mi queja triste
abandonada en medio de la tierra infinita!

Se muere el universo de una calma agonía
sin la fiesta del sol o el crepúsculo verde.
Agoniza Saturno como una pena mía,
la tierra es una fruta negra que el cielo muerde.

Y por la vastedad del vacío van ciegas
las nubes de la tarde, como barcas perdidas
que escondieran estrellas rotas en sus bodegas.

Y la muerte del mundo cae sobre mi vida.

I Am Afraid

I'm afraid. The evening is gray and the sadness
of the sky opens like the mouth of a corpse.
My heart has a weeping of princess
forgotten at the bottom of a deserted palace.

I'm afraid. And I feel so tired and small
that I reflect the evening without meditating on her.
(In my sick head a dream may not fit
just as a star has not fit in the sky.)

Even so a question exists in my eyes
and there is a shout in my mouth that my mouth doesn't shout.
There's no ear on earth that hears my sad bemoaning
abandoned in the middle of the infinite earth!

The universe dies from a calm agony
without the feast of the sun or the green twilight.
Saturn agonizes like a sorrow of mine,
Earth is a black fruit that the sky bites.

And through the vastness of the emptiness go
blindly the evening clouds like lost boats
that would hide broken stars in their holds.

And the death of the world falls over my life.

Ventana al camino

WINDOW ON THE ROAD

Entre los surcos tu cuerpo moreno
es un racimo que a la tierra llega.
Torna los ojos, mírate los senos,
son dos semillas ácidas y ciegas.

Tu carne es tierra que será madura
cuando el otoño te tienda las manos,
y el surco que será tu sepultura
temblará, temblará, como un humano

al recibir tus carnes y tus huesos
—rosas de pulpa con rosas de cal:
rosas que en el primero de los besos
vibraron como un vaso de cristal—.

La palabra de qué concepto pleno
será tu cuerpo? No lo he de saber!
Torna los ojos, mírate los senos,
tal vez no alcanzarás a florecer.

Peasant Woman

Among the furrows your brown body
in a cluster reaches to the earth.
Shift your eyes, look at your breasts,
they are two sour and blind seeds.

Your flesh is earth that will be ripe
when autumn extends its hands to you,
and the furrow that'll be your burial place
would shudder, will shudder, like a human

on receiving your flesh and your bones,
—roses of pulp with roses of lime:
roses that in the first of the kisses
vibrated like a crystal glass—.

The word of what whole concept
will your body be? I shall never know!
Turn your eyes, look at your breasts,
maybe you will not come to flower.

Agua dormida

Quiero saltar al agua para caer al cielo.

Water, Asleep

I want to leap into the water to fall on the sky.

SINFONÍA DE LA TRILLA

Sacude las épicas eras
un loco viento festival.
                    Ah yeguayeguaa!...
Como un botón en primavera
se abre un relincho de cristal.

Revienta la espiga gallarda
bajo las patas vigorosas.
                    Ah yeguayeguaa!...
Por aumentar la zalagarda
trillarían las mariposas!

Maduros trigos amarillos,
campos expertos en donar.
                    Ah yeguayeguaa!...
Hombres de corazón sencillo.
Qué más podemos esperar?

Éste es el fruto de tu ciencia,
varón de la mano callosa.
                    Ah yeguayeguaa!...
Sólo por falta de paciencia
las copihueras no dan rosas!

Sol que cayó a racimos sobre el llano,
ámbar del sol, quiero adorarte en todo:
en el oro del trigo y de las manos
que lo hicieran gavillas y recodos.

SYMPHONY OF THE THRESHING

A crazy festival wind
shakes the epic eras.
                    Gee up, maremaree!...
Like a bud in spring
a neigh of crystal opens.

The elegant spike bursts
under the vigorous hooves.
                    Gee up, maremaree!...
To increase the boisterous joy
the butterflies would thresh!

Ripe yellow wheat,
fields skilled at giving.
                    Gee up, maremaree!...
Men of simple heart.
What more can we expect?

This is the fruit of your science,
gentle man of the calloused hand.
                    Gee up, maremaree!...
Only for lack of patience
do Chilean bellflowers yield no roses.

Sun that fell in clusters over the plain,
amber of the sun, I want to adore you in everything:
in the gold of the wheat and of the hands
that'd shape it in sheaves and curves.

Ámbar del sol, quiero divinizarte
en la flor, en el grano y en el vino.
Amor sólo me alcanza para amarte:
para divinizarte, hazme divino!

Que la tierra florezca en mis acciones
como en el jugo de oro de las viñas,
que perfume el dolor de mis canciones
como un fruto olvidado en la campiña.

Que trascienda mi carne a sembradura
ávida de brotar por todas partes,
que mis arterias lleven agua pura,
agua que canta cuando se reparte!

Yo quiero estar desnudo en las gavillas,
pisado por los cascos enemigos,
yo quiero abrirme y entregar semillas
de pan: yo quiero ser de tierra y trigo!

Yo di licores rojos y dolientes
cuando trilló el Amor mis avenidas:
ahora daré licores de vertiente
y aromaré los valles con mi herida.

Campo, dame tus aguas y tus rocas,
entiérrame en tus surcos, o recoge
mi vida en las canciones de tu boca
como un grano de trigo de tus trojes...

Dulcifica mis labios con tus mieles
campo de los recónditos panales!

Amber of the sun, of you I want to make a god
in the flower, in the grain and in the wine.
I only have love enough to love you:
to make a god of yourself, make me divine!

Let the land flower in my actions
as in the golden juice of the vineyards,
let it scent the pain of my songs
like a fruit forgotten in the fields.

Let my flesh transcend into sowing,
eager to sprout everywhere,
let my arteries carry pure water,
water that sings when shared!

I want to be naked among the sheaves,
trodden down by enemy helmets,
I want to open myself and hand over seeds
of bread: I want to be of soil and wheat!

I yielded red and aching liquors
when Love threshed my avenues:
now I'll yield liquors of the slopes
and scent the valleys with my wound.

Field, give me your waters and your rocks,
bury me in your furrows, or gather
my life in the songs from your mouth
like a grain of wheat from your granaries…

Sweeten my lips with your honeys,
field of the hidden honeycombs!

———

Perfúmame a manzanas y laureles,
desgráname en los últimos trigales...

Lléname el corazón de cascabeles,
campo de los lebreles pastorales!

Rechinan por las carreteras
los carros de vientres fecundos.
                    Ah yeguayeguaa!...

La llamarada de las eras
es la cabellera del mundo!

Va un grito de bronce removiendo
las bestias que trillan sin tregua
en un remolino tremendo...
                    Ah yeguayeguaa!...

Scent me with apples and laurel,
shuck me in the last wheat fields...

Fill my heart with small round bells,
field of the countryside greyhounds!

They squeak along the back roads
the fecund belly carts.

                Gee up, maremaree!...

The flare of the eras
is the hair of the world!

A shout of bronze goes stirring
the beasts that thresh without rest
in a colossal whirlwind...

                Gee up, maremaree!...

La dentellada del mar muerde
la abierta pulpa de la costa
donde se estrella el agua verde
contra la tierra silenciosa.

Parado cielo y lejanía.
El horizonte, como un brazo,
rodea la fruta encendida
del sol cayendo en el ocaso.

Frente a la furia del mar son
inútiles todos los sueños.
Para qué decir la canción
de un corazón que es tan pequeño?

Sin embargo es tan vasto el cielo
y rueda el tiempo, sin embargo.
Tenderse y dejarse llevar
por este viento azul y amargo!...

Desgranado viento del mar,
sigue besándome la cara.
Arrástrame, viento del mar,
adonde nadie me esperara!

A la tierra más pobre y dura
llévame, viento, entre tus alas,
así como llevas a veces
las semillas de las hierbas malas.

SOUTHERN BEACH

The chewing jaws of the sea bite
the open pulp of the coast
where the green water crashes
against the silent earth.

Standing sky and distance.
The horizon, like an arm,
surrounds the lit-up fruit
of the sun falling into the dusk.

Facing the fury of the sea
all dreams are futile.
Why relate the song
of a heart that's so small?

Nevertheless, the sky is so vast
and time, nonetheless, rolls on.
To lie down and let oneself be carried
by this blue and bitter wind!...

Shelled wind of the sea,
go on kissing my face.
Drag me, wind of the sea,
where no one would wait for me!

To the most poor and hard earth
carry me, wind, between your wings,
just as sometimes you carry
the seeds of the bad grasses.

Ellas quieren rincones húmedos,
surcos abiertos, ellas quieren
crecer como todas las hierbas:
yo sólo quiero que me lleves!

Allá estaré como aquí estoy:
adonde vaya estaré siempre
con el deseo de partir
y con las manos en la frente...

Esa es la pequeña canción,
arrullada en un vasto sueño.
Para qué decir la canción
si el corazón es tan pequeño?

Pequeño frente al horizonte
y frente al mar enloquecido.
Si Dios gimiera en esta playa,
nadie oiría sus gemidos!

A mordiscos de sal y espuma
borra el mar mis últimos pasos...

La marea desata ahora
su cinturón, en el ocaso.

Y una bandada raya el cielo
como una nube de flechazos...

They seek damp corners,
open furrows, they want
to grow like all the weeds:
I only want you to carry me!

I will be there as I am here:
wherever I go I'll always
desire to take my leave
with my hand on my brow...

That's the small song,
lulled to sleep in a vast dream.
Why even say the song
if the heart is so small?

Small facing the horizon,
and facing the maddened sea.
If God groaned on this beach
no one would hear his groans!

With bites of salt and foam
the sea erases my last steps...

Now the tide unleashes
its belt, in the sunset.

And a flock lines the sky
like a cloud of arrows...

MANCHA EN TIERRAS DE COLOR

Patio de esta tierra, luminoso patio
tendido a la orilla del río y del mar.

Inclinado sobre la boca del pozo
del fondo del pozo me veo brotar

como en una instantánea de sesenta cobres
distante y movida. Fotógrafo pobre,

el agua retrata mi camisa suelta
y mi pelo de hebras negras y revueltas.

Un alado piño de pájaros sube
como una escalera de seda, una nube.

Y, asomando detrás de la cerca sencilla,
cabeza amarilla, como maravilla,

como el corazón de la siesta en la trilla
rubia como el alma de las manzanillas,

veo a veces, gloria del paisaje seco,
la cabeza rubia de Laura Pacheco.

Stain on Lands of Color

Courtyard of this earth, luminous courtyard
lying upon the shore of the river and the sea.

Leaning over the mouth of the well
from the bottom of the well I see myself burst

as in a distant and blurred snapshot
of sixty coppers. Poor photographer,

the water photographs my loose shirt
and my hair of black and snarled strands.

A winged crowd of birds rises
like a ladder of silk, one cloud.

And, poking out from behind the simple fence,
yellow head, like wonder,

like the heart of the siesta in the threshing,
blond as the soul of the chamomile

—I sometimes see—glory of the dry countryside,
the blond head of Laura Pacheco.

Poema en diez versos

Era mi corazón un ala viva y turbia
y pavorosa ala de anhelo.

Era Primavera sobre los campos verdes.
Azul era la altura y era esmeralda el suelo.

Ella—la que me amaba—se murió en Primavera.
Recuerdo aún sus ojos de paloma en desvelo.

Ella—la que me amaba—cerró los ojos. Tarde.
Tarde de campo, azul. Tarde de alas y vuelos.

Ella—la que me amaba—se murió en Primavera.
Y se llevó la Primavera al cielo.

Poem in Ten Verses

My heart was a wing, alive and roiled,
and a frightening wing of longing.

Spring was in the green fields.
The heights were blue and the ground emerald.

She—the one who loved me—died in spring.
I remember still her eyes of sleepy dove.

She—the one who loved me—closed her eyes. Evening.
Blue countryside evening. Evening of wings and flights.

She—the one who loved me—died in spring.
And carried the spring to the sky.

El pueblo

La sombra de este monte protector y propicio,
como una manta indiana fresca y rural me cubre:
bebo el azul del cielo por mis ojos sin vicio
como un ternero mama la leche de las ubres.

Al pie de la colina se extiende el pueblo y siento,
sin quererlo, el rodar de los tranways urbanos:
una iglesia se eleva para clavar el viento,
pero el muy vagabundo se le va de las manos.

Pueblo, eres triste y gris. Tienes las calles largas,
y un olor de almacén por tus calles pasea.
El agua de tus pozos la encuentro más amarga.
Las almas de tus hombres me parecen más feas.

No saben la belleza de un surtidor que canta,
ni del que la trasvasa floreciendo un concepto.
Sin detenerse, como el agua en la garganta,
desde sus corazones se va el verso perfecto.

El pueblo es gris y triste. Si estoy ausente pienso
que la ausencia parece que lo acercara a mí.
Regreso, y hasta el cielo tiene un bostezo inmenso.
Y crece en mi alma un odio, como el de antes, intenso.

Pero ella vive aquí.

The Town

The shadow of this sheltering and auspicious mountain,
like a cool and rustic Indian blanket, covers me:
I drink the blue of the sky through my eyes without vice,
as a calf does the milk of the udders.

The town stretches to the foot of the hill and I feel,
without wanting to, the roll of the urban tramways:
a church rises to nail fast the wind,
but ever the wanderer it escapes her hands.

Town, you are sad and gray. You have long streets
and through your streets roams a smell of warehouse.
I find the water from your wells most bitter.
The souls of your men seem most ugly.

They don't know the beauty of a pump that sings,
nor of he who pours forth water, blossoming a concept.
With no stopping, like water in the throat,
the perfect poem leaves their hearts.

The town is gray and sad. If I'm absent, I think
my absence will bring it closer to me.
I return, and even the sky issues an immense yawn.
And as before an intense hatred grows in my soul.

But she lives here.

Pelleas y Melisanda

PELLEAS AND MELISANDA

MELISANDA

Su cuerpo es una hostia fina, mínima y leve.
Tiene azules los ojos y las manos de nieve.

En el parque los árboles parecen congelados,
los pájaros en ellos se detienen cansados.

Sus trenzas rubias tocan el agua dulcemente
como dos brazos de oro brotados de la fuente.

Zumba el vuelo perdido de las lechuzas ciegas.
Melisanda se pone de rodillas y ruega.

Los árboles se inclinan hasta tocar su frente.
Los pájaros se alejan en la tarde doliente.

Melisanda, la dulce, llora junto a la fuente.

MELISANDA

Her body is a slender wafer, so small and light.
She has blue eyes and hands of snow.

In the park the trees appear frozen,
in them the weary birds stop.

Her blond braids sweetly touch the water
like two golden arms sprouted from the fountain.

The lost flight of the blind owls buzzes.
Melisanda falls to her knees—and begs.

The trees lean down until they touch her brow.
The birds retreat in the aching evening.

Melisanda, the sweet, cries beside the fountain.

El encantamiento

Melisanda, la dulce, se ha extraviado de ruta:
Pelleas, lirio azul de un jardín imperial,
se la lleva en los brazos como un cesto de fruta.

The Enchantment

Melisanda, the sweet, has gotten lost on the path:
Pelleas, blue lily of an imperial garden,
carries her in his arms, like a basket of fruit.

El coloquio maravillado

Pelleas

Iba yo por la senda, tú venías por ella,
mi amor cayó en tus brazos, tu amor tembló en los míos.
Desde entonces mi cielo de noche tuvo estrellas
y para recogerlas se hizo tu vida un río.

Para ti cada roca que tocarán mis manos
ha de ser manantial, aroma, fruta y flor.

Melisanda

Para ti cada espiga debe apretar su grano
y en cada espiga debe desgranarse mi amor.

Pelleas

Me impedirás, en cambio, que yo mire la senda
cuando llegue la muerte para dejarla trunca.

Melisanda

Te cubrirán mis ojos como una doble venda.

Pelleas

Me hablarás de un camino que no termine nunca.
La música que escondo para encantarse huye
lejos de la canción que borbota y resalta:
como una vía láctea desde mi pecho fluye.

The Wondrous Conversation

Pelleas

I was on the path, you came along it,
my love fell in your arms, your love trembled in mine.
From then on, my night sky filled with stars
and to gather them your life became a river.

For you, every rock that my hands will touch
must be spring, fragrance, fruit and flower.

Melisanda

For you each spike must clutch its grain
and in each spike my love must rip away its grain.

Pelleas

You'll keep me, in return, from watching the path
when death arrives to thwart it.

Melisanda

My eyes will cover you like a double bandage.

Pelleas

You'll speak to me of a road that never ends.
The music I hide to enchant you flees
far from the song that mutters and stands out:
as if a milky way streams from my chest.

Melisanda

En tus brazos se enredan las estrellas más altas.
Tengo miedo. Perdóname no haber llegado antes.

Pelleas

Una sonrisa tuya borra todo un pasado:
guarden tus labios dulces lo que ya está distante.

Melisanda

En un beso sabrás todo lo que he callado.

Pelleas

Tal vez no sepa entonces conocer tu caricia,
porque en las venas mías tu ser se habrá fundido.

Melisanda

Cuando yo muerda un fruto tú sabrás su delicia.

Pelleas

Cuando cierres los ojos me quedaré dormido.

Melisanda

In your arms the highest stars get tangled up.
I'm afraid. Forgive me, I could come no earlier.

Pelleas

One of your smiles erases an entire past:
may your sweet lips keep what's now far away.

Melisanda

With a kiss you'll know all I've kept quiet.

Pelleas

Perhaps then I won't know how to know your caress,
because in these veins of mine your being will have melted.

Melisanda

When I bite into a fruit you'll know its pleasure.

Pelleas

When you close your eyes I'll fall asleep.

La cabellera

Pesada, espesa y rumorosa,
en la ventana del castillo
la cabellera de la Amada
es un lampadario amarillo.

—Tus manos blancas en mi boca.
—Mi frente en tu frente lunada.
Pelleas, ebrio, tambalea
bajo la selva perfumada.

—Melisanda, un lebrel aúlla
por los caminos de la aldea.
—Siempre que aúllan los lebreles
me muero de espanto, Pelleas.

—Melisanda, un corcel galopa
cerca del bosque de laureles.
—Tiemblo, Pelleas, en la noche
cuando galopan los corceles.

—Pelleas, alguien me ha tocado
la sien con una mano fina.
—Sería un beso de tu amado
o el ala de una golondrina.

En la ventana del castillo
en un lampadario amarillo
la milagrosa cabellera.

THE HEAD OF HAIR

Heavy, thick and murmuring,
in the window of the castle
the hair of the Loved One
is a yellow candelabrum.

—Your white hands in my mouth.
—My brow on your half-moon brow.
Pelleas, drunk, staggers
under the perfumed forest.

—Melisanda, a greyhound howls
through the streets of the village.
—Whenever the greyhounds howl
I die of fright, Pelleas.

—Melisanda, a steed gallops
near the laurel woods.
—I tremble, Pelleas, in the night
when the steeds gallop.

—Pelleas, someone has touched
my temple with a delicate hand.
—It might be a kiss from your beloved
or the wing of a swallow.

In the window of the castle
is a yellow candelabrum
the miraculous hair.

Ebrio, Pelleas enloquece:
su corazón también quisiera
ser una boca que la bese.

Drunk, Pelleas maddens:
his heart also would be
a mouth that kisses her.

La muerte de Melisanda

A la sombra de los laureles
Melisanda se está muriendo.

Se morirá su cuerpo leve.
Enterrarán su dulce cuerpo.

Juntarán sus manos de nieve.
Dejarán sus ojos abiertos

para que alumbren a Pelleas
hasta después que se haya muerto.

A la sombra de los laureles
Melisanda muere en silencio.

Por ella llorará la fuente
un llanto trémulo y eterno.

Por ella orarán los cipreses
arrodillados bajo el viento.

Habrá galope de corceles,
lunarios ladridos de perros.

A la sombra de los laureles
Melisanda se está muriendo.

Por ella el sol en el castillo
se apagará como un enfermo.

The Death of Melisanda

In the shadow of laurels
Melisanda is dying.

Her slight body will die.
They'll bury her sweet body.

They'll place together her hands of snow.
They'll leave her eyes open

so they light up Pelleas
even after he has died.

In the shadow of the laurels
Melisanda dies in silence.

For her the fountain will cry,
a weeping tremulous and eternal.

For her the cypresses will pray
kneeling under the wind.

There will be galloping of steeds,
lunar barking of dogs.

In the shadow of laurels
Melisanda is dying.

For her the sun in the castle,
like a patient, will die away.

Por ella morirá Pelleas
cuando la lleven al entierro.

Por ella vagará de noche,
moribundo por los senderos.

Por ella pisará las rosas,
perseguirá las mariposas
y dormirá en los cementerios.

Por ella, por ella, por ella
Pelleas, el príncipe, ha muerto.

For her Pelleas will die
when they carry her to the burial.

For her he'll wander at night,
dying along the trails.

For her he'll trample the roses,
chase the butterflies
and sleep in the cemeteries.

For her, for her, for her
Pelleas, the prince, has died.

Canción de los amantes muertos

Ella era bella y era buena.

> Perdonalá, Señor!

Él era dulce y era triste.

> Perdonaló, Señor!

Se dormía en sus brazos blancos
como una abeja en una flor.

> Perdonaló, Señor!

Amaba las dulces canciones,
ella era una dulce canción!

> Perdonalá, Señor!

Cuando hablaba era como si alguien
hubiera llorado en su voz.

> Perdonaló, Señor!

Ella decía: —"Tengo miedo.
Oigo una voz en lo lejano".

> Perdonalá, Señor!

Él decía: —"Tu pequeñita
mano en mis labios".

> Perdonaló, Señor!

Song of the Dead Lovers

She was beautiful and was good.

    Forgive her, my Lord!

He was sweet and was sad.

    My Lord, forgive him!

He'd fall asleep in her white arms
like a bee on a flower.

    Forgive him, Lord!

He loved sweet songs,
she was a sweet song!

    Lord, forgive her!

When she'd speak it was as if someone
had wept inside her voice.

    Forgive him, Lord!

She'd say: "I'm afraid.
I hear a voice in the distance."

    Lord, forgive her!

He'd say: "Your little
hand on my lips."

    Forgive him, my Lord!

———

Miraban juntos las estrellas,
no hablaban de amor.

Cuando moría una mariposa
lloraban los dos.

Perdonalós, Señor!

Ella era bella y era buena.
Él era dulce y era triste.
Murieron del mismo dolor.

Perdonalós,
Perdonalós,

Perdonalós, Señor!

Together they'd watch the stars.
They wouldn't speak of love.
When a butterfly died
they'd both cry.

        Forgive them, Lord!

She was beautiful and good.
He was sweet and sad.
They died of the same ache.

Forgive them,
Forgive them,

        Forgive them, My Lord!

FINAL

END

Fueron creadas por mí estas palabras
con sangre mía, con dolores míos,
fueron creadas!

Yo lo comprendo, amigos, yo lo comprendo todo.
Se mezclaron voces ajenas a las mías,
yo lo comprendo, amigos!
Como si yo quisiera volar y a mí llegaran
en ayuda las alas de las aves,
todas las alas,
así vinieron estas palabras extranjeras
a desatar la oscura ebriedad de mi alma.

Es el alba, y parece
que no se me apretaran las angustias
en tan terribles nudos en torno a la garganta.
Y sin embargo,
fueron creadas,
con sangre mía, con dolores míos,
fueron creadas por mí estas palabras!

Palabras para la alegría
cuando era mi corazón
una corola de llamas,
palabras del dolor que clava,
de los instintos que remuerden,
de los impulsos que amenazan,
de los infinitos deseos,
de las inquietudes amargas,
palabras del amor, que en mi vida florecen
como una tierra roja llena de umbelas blancas.

These words were created by me
with blood of mine, with pains of mine
they were created!

I understand, friends, I grasp it all.
Voices not my own mingled with mine,
I get it, friends!
As if I wanted to fly, the wings of birds
arrived to help me,
all the wings,
and so these foreign words came
to unleash the dark drunkenness of my soul.

It is dawn, and it seems
that my inquietudes won't tighten
in such terrible knots around my throat.
And nevertheless,
they were created,
with my blood, with my pains,
these words were created by me!

Words for the joy
when my heart
was a corolla of flames,
words of the pain that drives nails,
of the instincts that gnaw,
of the impulses that threaten,
of the infinite desires,
of the bitter disquietudes,
words from love, which in my life flower
like a red land filled with round clusters of white petals.

———

No cabían en mí. Nunca cupieron.
De niño mi dolor fue grito
y mi alegría fue silencio.

Después los ojos
olvidaron las lágrimas
barridas por el viento del corazón de todos.

Ahora, decidme, amigos,
dónde esconder aquella aguda
furia de los sollozos.

Decidme, amigos, dónde
esconder el silencio, para que nunca nadie
lo sintiera con los oídos o con los ojos.

Vinieron las palabras, y mi corazón,
incontenible como un amanecer,
se rompió en las palabras y se apegó a su vuelo,
y en sus fugas heroicas lo llevan y lo arrastran,
abandonado y loco, y olvidado bajo ellas
como un pájaro muerto, debajo de sus alas.

They didn't fit within me. They never fit.
In childhood my pain was a cry
and my joy was silence.

Later my eyes
forgot the tears
swept by the wind of the heart of everyone.

Tell me now, friends,
where to hide that shrill
fury of the sobs.

Friends, tell me where
to hide the silence, so no one ever
sensed it with their ears or with their eyes.

The words came, and my heart,
uncontainable as a dawn,
cracked in the words and attached to their flight,
and in their heroic escape they carry it and they drag it,
abandoned and crazy, and forgotten below them
like a dead bird, under their wings.

About the Author

Pablo Neruda was born Neftalí Ricardo Reyes Basoalto in Parral, Chile, in 1904. He served as consul in Burma and held diplomatic posts in various East Asian and European countries. In 1945, a few years after he joined the Communist Party, Neruda was elected to the Chilean Senate. Shortly thereafter, when Chile's political climate took a sudden turn to the right, Neruda fled to Mexico, and he lived as an exile for several years. He later established a permanent home at Isla Negra. In 1970 he was appointed as Chile's ambassador to France, and in 1971 he was awarded the Nobel Prize in Literature. Neruda died in 1973.

William O'Daly's translations from the Spanish include eight previous books of poetry by Pablo Neruda, all published with Copper Canyon Press. His collection *Water Ways* (Folded Word Press), with prose and photos by JS Graustein, was published in 2017. Another book of poems, *Yarrow and Smoke,* will appear in 2018 from Folded Word. His chapbooks are *The Whale in the Web* (Copper Canyon) and *The Road to Isla Negra* (Folded Word). As a 2006 Quill Award finalist for his Neruda translation *Still Another Day* (*Aún*), he was profiled by Mike Leonard for *The Today Show.* O'Daly is a National Endowment for the Arts Fellow, and his poems, translations, essays, and reviews appear widely in journals and anthologies.

Poetry is vital to language and living. Since 1972, Copper Canyon Press has published extraordinary poetry from around the world to engage the imaginations and intellects of readers, writers, booksellers, librarians, teachers, students, and donors.

WE ARE GRATEFUL FOR THE MAJOR SUPPORT PROVIDED BY:

4
CULTURE

Lannan

TO LEARN MORE ABOUT UNDERWRITING
COPPER CANYON PRESS TITLES,
PLEASE CALL 360-385-4925 EXT. 103

WE ARE GRATEFUL FOR THE MAJOR SUPPORT PROVIDED BY:

Anonymous

Jill Baker and Jeffrey Bishop

Donna and Matt Bellew

John Branch

Diana Broze

Sarah and Tim Cavanaugh

Janet and Les Cox

Mimi Gardner Gates

Linda Gerrard and Walter Parsons

Gull Industries, Inc. on behalf of
Ruth and William True

The Trust of Warren A. Gummow

Steven Myron Holl

Phil Kovacevich and Eric Wechsler

Lakeside Industries, Inc.
on behalf of Jeanne Marie Lee

Maureen Lee and Mark Busto

Rhoady Lee and Alan Gartenhaus

Ellie Mathews and Carl Youngmann
as The North Press

Anne O'Donnell and John Phillips

Petunia Charitable Fund and
advisor Elizabeth Hebert

Suzie Rapp and Mark Hamilton

Joseph C. Roberts

Jill and Bill Ruckelshaus

Cynthia Lovelace Sears and
Frank Buxton

Kim and Jeff Seely

Catherine Eaton Skinner and
David Skinner

Dan Waggoner

Austin Walters

Barbara and Charles Wright

The dedicated interns and
faithful volunteers of
Copper Canyon Press

The Chinese character for poetry is made up of two parts:
"word" and "temple." It also serves as pressmark for
Copper Canyon Press.

The poems are set in Sabon.
Book design and composition by Phil Kovacevich.
Printed on archival-quality paper.